Poems

Mary Baker Eddy

Contents

PREFACE	7
OLD MAN OF THE MOUNTAIN	9
CONSTANCY	11
MOTHER'S EVENING PRAYER	11
LOVE	12
I'M SITTING ALONE	14
THE UNITED STATES TO GREAT BRITAIN	15
CHRIST MY REFUGE	16
"*FEED MY SHEEP*"	17
THE VALLEY CEMETERY	18
UPWARD	20
THE OAK ON THE MOUNTAIN'S SUMMIT	21
WOMAN'S RIGHTS	21
THE NEW CENTURY	22
TO MY ABSENT BROTHER	23
SIGNS OF THE HEART	24
FLOWERS	25
TO THE OLD YEAR--1865	26
INVOCATION FOR 1868	28
CHRISTMAS MORN	29
EASTER MORN	30
RESOLUTIONS FOR THE DAY	31
O FOR THY WINGS, SWEET BIRD!	32
COME THOU	34
WISH AND ITEM	35
DEDICATION OF A TEMPERANCE HALL	36
LINES	37
TO THE SUNDAY SCHOOL CHILDREN	38
HOPE	39
TO ETTA	40
NEVERMORE	41
MEETING OF MY DEPARTED MOTHER AND HUSBAND	42
ISLE OF WIGHT	44
SPRING	45
JUNE	46
RONDELET	47
AUTUMN	48
ALPHABET AND BAYONET	49
THE COUNTRY-SEAT	50
TO ELLEN. "SING ME THAT SONG!"	52
LINES, ON VISITING PINE GROVE CEMETERY	53
A VERSE	55
TRUTH	55
"*THE LIBERTY BELLS*"	56
"*MEMENTO*"	58
COMMUNION HYMN	59
LAUS DEO!	60
OUR NATIONAL THANKSGIVING HYMN	61
SATISFIED	62

POEMS

BY
Mary Baker Eddy

POEMS by

MARY BAKER EDDY

Author of "Science and Health with Key

to the Scriptures"

PREFACE

The poems garnered up in this little volume were written at different periods in the life of the author, dating from her early girlhood up to recent years. They were not written with a view of making a book, each poem being the spontaneous outpouring of a deeply poetic nature and called forth by some experience that claimed her attention.

The "Old Man of the Mountain," for instance, was written while the author was contemplating this lofty New Hampshire crag, whose rugged outlines resemble the profile of a human face. Inspired by the grandeur of this masterpiece of nature's handiwork, and looking "up through nature, unto nature's God," the poem began to take form in her thought, and alighting from her carriage, she seated herself by the roadside and began to write. Some tourists who were passing, and who made her acquaintance, asked her what she was writing, and she replied by reading the poem to them. They were so pleased with it that each requested a copy, which was subsequently mailed to them. Similar requests continued to reach the author for years afterward, until the poem finally found its way into print, appearing, together with "The Valley Cemetery," in a book "Gems for You," published in Manchester, N. H., in 1850, and again in Boston, in 1856.

The poem on the "Dedication of a Temperance Hall," in Lynn, Mass., in 1866, was written for that occasion, and was sung by the audience as a dedicatory hymn. "The Liberty Bells" appeared in a Lynn, Mass., newspaper, under the date of February 3, 1865. A note from the author, which was published with the poem, read as follows:

"MR. EDITOR:--In 1835 a mob in Boston (although Boston has since been the pioneer of anti-slavery) dispersed a meeting of the Female Anti-Slavery Society, and assailed the person of William Lloyd Garrison with such fury that the city authorities could protect him nowhere but in the walls of a jail. To-day, by order of Governor Andrew, the bells are ringing to celebrate the passing of a resolution in Congress prohibiting slavery in the United States."

All of the author's best-known hymns are included in this collection, as well as many poems written in girlhood and during the years she resided in Lynn, Mass., and which appeared in various publications of that day. Among her earliest poems are "Upward," "Resolutions for the Day," "Autumn" (written in a maple grove), "Alphabet and Bayonet," and "The Country-Seat" (written while visiting a family friend in the beautiful suburbs of Boston); yet, even these are characterized by the same lofty trend of thought that reached its fulness in her later productions.

In May, 1910, Mrs. Eddy requested her publisher to prepare a few bound volumes of her poems, for private distribution. When this became known to her friends, they urged her to allow a popular edition to be issued, to which she assented. With grateful acknowledgment, therefore, of this permission, this little volume is presented to the public, in the hope that these gems of purest thought from this spiritually-minded author will prove a joy to the heavy laden and a balm to the weary heart.

ADAM H. DICKEY.

CHESTNUT HILL, MASS., September 24, 1910.

POEMS

OLD MAN OF THE MOUNTAIN

Gigantic sire, unfallen still thy crest!
Primeval dweller where the wild winds rest,
Beyond the ken of mortal e'er to tell
What power sustains thee in thy rock-bound cell.

Or if, when first creation vast began,
And far the universal fiat ran,
"Let there be light"--from chaos dark set free,

Ye rose, a monument of Deity,

Proud from yon cloud-crowned height to look henceforth
On insignificance that peoples earth,
Recalling oft the bitter draft which turns
The mind to meditate on what it learns.

Stern, passionless, no soul those looks betray;
Though kindred rocks, to sport at mortal clay--
Much as the chisel of the sculptor's art
"Plays round the head, but comes not to the heart."

Ah, who can fathom thee! Ambitious man,
Like a trained falcon in the Gallic van,
Guided and led, can never reach to thee
With all the strength of weakness--vanity!

Great as thou art, and paralleled by none,
Admired by all, still art thou drear and lone!
The moon looks down upon thine exiled height;
The stars, so cold, so glitteringly bright,

On wings of morning gladly flit away,
Yield to the sun's more genial, mighty ray;
The white waves kiss the murmuring rill--
But thy deep silence is unbroken still.

CONSTANCY

When starlight blends with morning's hue,
I miss thee as the flower the dew!
When noonday's length'ning shadows flee,
I think of thee, I think of thee!

With evening, memories reappear--
I watch thy chair, and wish thee here;
Till sleep sets drooping fancy free
To dream of thee, to dream of thee!

Since first we met, in weal or woe
It hath been thus; and must be so
Till bursting bonds our spirits part
And Love divine doth fill my heart.

Written many years ago.

MOTHER'S EVENING PRAYER

O gentle presence, peace and joy and power;
O Life divine, that owns each waiting hour,
Thou Love that guards the nestling's faltering flight!
Keep Thou my child on upward wing tonight.

Love is our refuge; only with mine eye
Can I behold the snare, the pit, the fall:
His habitation high is here, and nigh,
His arm encircles me, and mine, and all.

O make me glad for every scalding tear,
For hope deferred, ingratitude, disdain!
Wait, and love more for every hate, and fear
No ill,--since God is good, and loss is gain.

Beneath the shadow of His mighty wing;
In that sweet secret of the narrow way,
Seeking and finding, with the angels sing:
"Lo, I am with you alway,"--watch and pray.

No snare, no fowler, pestilence or pain;
No night drops down upon the troubled breast,
When heaven's aftersmile earth's tear-drops gain,
And mother finds her home and heav'nly rest.

LOVE

Brood o'er us with Thy shelt'ring wing,
'Neath which our spirits blend
Like brother birds, that soar and sing,
And on the same branch bend.
The arrow that doth wound the dove
Darts not from those who watch and love.

If thou the bending reed wouldst break
By thought or word unkind,
Pray that his spirit you partake,
Who loved and healed mankind:
Seek holy thoughts and heavenly strain,
That make men one in love remain.

Learn, too, that wisdom's rod is given
For faith to kiss, and know;
That greetings glorious from high heaven,
Whence joys supernal flow,
Come from that Love, divinely near,
Which chastens pride and earth-born fear,
Through God, who gave that word of might
Which swelled creation's lay:
"Let there be light, and there was light."
What chased the clouds away?
'Twas Love whose finger traced aloud
A bow of promise on the cloud.

Thou to whose power our hope we give,
Free us from human strife.
Fed by Thy love divine we live,
For Love alone is Life;
And life most sweet, as heart to heart
Speaks kindly when we meet and part.

I'M SITTING ALONE

I'm sitting alone where the shadows fall
In somber groups at the vesper-call,
Where tear-dews of night seek the loving rose,
Her bosom to fill with mortal woes.

I'm waiting alone for the bridal hour
Of nymph and naiad from woodland bower;
Till vestal pearls that on leaflets lay,
Ravished with beauty the eye of day.

I'm watching alone o'er the starlit glow,
O'er the silv'ry moon and ocean flow;
And sketching in light the heaven of my youth--
Its starry hopes and its waves of truth.

I'm dreaming alone of its changeful sky--
What rainbows of rapture floated by!
Of a mother's love, that no words could speak
When parting the ringlets to kiss my cheek.

I'm thinking alone of a fair young bride,
The light of a home of love and pride;
How the glance of her husband's watchful eye
Turned to his star of idolatry.

I'm picturing alone a glad young face,
Upturned to his mother's in playful grace;
And the unsealed fountains of grief and joy
That gushed at the birth of that beautiful boy.

I'm weeping alone that the vision is fled,
The leaves all faded, the fruitage shed,
And wishing this earth more gifts from above,
Our reason made right and hearts all love.

Lynn, Mass., *September 3, 1866*.

THE UNITED STATES TO GREAT BRITAIN

Hail, brother! fling thy banner
To the billows and the breeze;
We proffer thee warm welcome
With our hand, though not our knees.

Lord of the main and manor!
Thy palm, in ancient day,
Didst rock the country's cradle
That wakes thy laureate's lay.

The hoar fight is forgotten;
Our eagle, like the dove,
Returns to bless a bridal
Betokened from above.

List, brother! angels whisper
To Judah's sceptered race,--
"Thou of the self-same spirit,
Allied by nations' grace,

"Wouldst cheer the hosts of heaven;
For Anglo-Israel, lo!
Is marching under orders;
His hand averts the blow."

Brave Britain, blest America!
Unite your battle-plan;
Victorious, all who live it,--
The love for God and man.

Boston Herald, Sunday, May 15, 1898.

CHRIST MY REFUGE

O'er waiting harpstrings of the mind
There sweeps a strain,
Low, sad, and sweet, whose measures bind
The power of pain,

And wake a white-winged angel throng
Of thoughts, illumed
By faith, and breathed in raptured song,
With love perfumed.

Then His unveiled, sweet mercies show
Life's burdens light.
I kiss the cross, and wake to know
A world more bright.

And o'er earth's troubled, angry sea
I see Christ walk,
And come to me, and tenderly,
Divinely talk.

Thus Truth engrounds me on the rock,
Upon Life's shore,
'Gainst which the winds and waves can shock,
Oh, nevermore!

From tired joy and grief afar,
And nearer Thee,--
Father, where Thine own children are,
I love to be.

My prayer, some daily good to do
To Thine, for Thee;
An offering pure of Love, whereto
God leadeth me.

"*FEED MY SHEEP*"

Shepherd, show me how to go
O'er the hillside steep,
How to gather, how to sow,--
How to feed Thy sheep;
I will listen for Thy voice,
Lest my footsteps stray;

I will follow and rejoice
All the rugged way.

Thou wilt bind the stubborn will,
Wound the callous breast,
Make self-righteousness be still,
Break earth's stupid rest.
Strangers on a barren shore,
Lab'ring long and lone,
We would enter by the door,
And Thou know'st Thine own;

So, when day grows dark and cold,
Tear or triumph harms,
Lead Thy lambkins to the fold,
Take them in Thine arms;
Feed the hungry, heal the heart,
Till the morning's beam;
White as wool, ere they depart,
Shepherd, wash them clean.

THE VALLEY CEMETERY

Ye soft sighing zephyrs through foliage and vine!
Ye echoing moans from the footsteps of time!
Break not on the silence, unless thou canst bear
A message from heaven--"No partings are there."

Here gloom hath enchantment in beauty's array,

And whispering voices are calling away--
Their wooings are soft as the vision more vain--
I would live in their empire, or die in their chain.

Here smileth the blossom and sunshine not dead--
Flowers fresh as the pang in the bosom that bled,--
Yes, constant as love that outliveth the grave,
And time cannot quench in oblivion's wave.

And thou, gentle cypress, in evergreen tears,
Art constant and hopeful though winter appears.
My heart hath thy verdure, it blossoms above;
Like thee, it endureth and liveth in love.

Ambition, come hither! These vaults will unfold
The sequel of power, of glory, or gold;
Then rush into life, and roll on with its tide,
And bustle and toil for its pomp and its pride.

The tired wings flitting through far crimson glow,
Which steepeth the trees when the day-god is low;
The voice of the night-bird must here send a thrill
To the heart of the leaves when the winds are all still.

'Mid graves do I hear the glad voices that swell,
And call to my spirit with seraphs to dwell;
They come with a breath from the verdant springtime,
And waken my joy, as in earliest prime.

Blest beings departed! Ye echoes at dawn!
O tell of their radiant home and its morn!
Then I'll think of its glory, and rest till I see
My loved ones in glory still waiting for me.

UPWARD

I've watched in the azure the eagle's proud wing,
His soaring majestic, and feathersome fling--
Careening in liberty higher and higher--
Like genius unfolding a quenchless desire.

Would a tear dim his eye, or pinion lose power
To gaze on the lark in her emerald bower?
When higher he soareth to compass his rest,
What vision so bright as the dream in his breast!

God's eye is upon him. He penciled his path
Whose omniscient notice the frail fledgling hath.
Though lightnings be lurid and earthquakes may shock,
He rides on the whirlwind or rests on the rock.

My course, like the eagle's, oh, still be it high,
Celestial the breezes that waft o'er its sky!
God's eye is upon me--I am not alone
When onward and upward and heavenward borne.

Written in early years.

THE OAK ON THE MOUNTAIN'S SUMMIT

Oh, mountain monarch, at whose feet I stand,--
Clouds to adorn thy brow, skies clasp thy hand,--
Nature divine, in harmony profound,
With peaceful presence hath begirt thee round.

And thou, majestic oak, from yon high place
Guard'st thou the earth, asleep in night's embrace,--
And from thy lofty summit, pouring down
Thy sheltering shade, her noonday glories crown?

Whate'er thy mission, mountain sentinel,
To my lone heart thou art a power and spell;
A lesson grave, of life, that teacheth me
To love the Hebrew figure of a tree.

Faithful and patient be my life as thine;
As strong to wrestle with the storms of time;
As deeply rooted in a soil of love;
As grandly rising to the heavens above.

WOMAN'S RIGHTS

Grave on her monumental pile;

She won from vice, by virtue's smile,
Her dazzling crown, her sceptered throne,
Affection's wreath, a happy home;

The right to worship deep and pure,
To bless the orphan, feed the poor;
Last at the cross to mourn her Lord,
First at the tomb to hear his word;

To fold an angel's wings below;
And hover o'er the couch of woe;
To nurse the Bethlehem babe so sweet,
The right to sit at Jesus' feet;

To form the bud for bursting bloom,
The hoary head with joy to crown;
In short, the right to work and pray,
"To point to heaven and lead the way."

Lynn, Mass., *May 6, 1876*.

THE NEW CENTURY

Thou God-crowned, patient century,
Thine hour hath come! Eternity
Draws nigh--and, beckoning from above,
One hundred years, aflame with Love,
Again shall bid old earth good-by--
And, lo, the light! far heaven is nigh!

New themes seraphic, Life divine,
And bliss that wipes the tears of time
Away, will enter, when they may,
And bask in one eternal day.

'Tis writ on earth, on leaf and flower:
Love hath one race, one realm, one power.
Dear God! how great, how good Thou art
To heal humanity's sore heart;
To probe the wound, then pour the balm--
A life perfected, strong and calm.
The dark domain of pain and sin
Surrenders--Love doth enter in,
And peace is won, and lost is vice:
Right reigns, and blood was not its price.

Pleasant View, Concord, N. H., *January, 1901*.

TO MY ABSENT BROTHER

Dwells there a shadow on thy brow--
A look that years impart?
Does there a thought of vanished hours
Come ever o'er thy heart?

Or give those earnest eyes yet back
An image of the soul,
Mirrored in truth, in light and joy,
Above the world's control?

So may their gaze be ever fraught
With utterance deep and strong,
Yielding a holy strength to right,
A stern rebuke to wrong!

Thy soul, upborne on wisdom's wings,
In brighter morn will find
Life hath a higher recompense
Than just to please mankind.

Supreme and omnipresent God,
Guide him in wisdom's way!
Give peaceful triumph to the truth,
Bid error melt away!

Lynn, Mass., *November 8, 1866*.

SIGNS OF THE HEART

Come to me, joys of heaven!
Breathe through the summer air
A balm--the long-lost leaven
Dissolving death, despair!
O little heart,
To me thou art
A sign that never can depart.

Come to me, peace on earth!

From out life's billowy sea,--
A wave of welcome birth,--
The Life that lives in Thee!
O Love divine,
This heart of Thine
Is all I need to comfort mine.

Come when the shadows fall,
And night grows deeply dark;
The barren brood, O call
With song of morning lark;
And from above,
Dear heart of Love,
Send us thy white-winged dove.

Pleasant View, Concord, N. H., 1899.

FLOWERS

Mirrors of morn
Whence the dewdrop is born,
Soft tints of the rainbow and skies--
Sisters of song,
What a shadowy throng
Around you in memory rise!

Far do ye flee,
From your green bowers free,
Fair floral apostles of love,

Sweetly to shed
Fragrance fresh round the dead,
And breath of the living above.

Flowers for the brave--
Be he monarch or slave,
Whose heart bore its grief and is still!
Flowers for the kind--
Aye, the Christians who wind
Wreaths for the triumphs o'er ill!

Pleasant View, Concord, N. H., *May 21, 1904*.

TO THE OLD YEAR--1865

Pass on, returnless year!
The track behind thee is with glory crowned;
The turf where thou hast trod is holy ground.
Pass proudly to thy bier!

Chill was thy midnight day,
While Justice grasped the sword to hold her throne,
And on her altar our loved Lincoln's own
Great willing heart did lay.

Thy purpose hath been won!
Thou point'st thy phantom finger, grim and cold,
To the dark record of our guilt unrolled,
And smiling, say'st, "'Tis done!

"This record I will bear
To the dim chambers of eternity--
The chain and charter I have lived to see
Purged by the cannon's prayer;

"Convulsion, carnage, war;
The pomp and tinsel of unrighteous power;
Bloated oppression in its awful hour,--
I, dying, dare abhor!"

One word, receding year,
Ere thou grow tremulous with shadowy night!
Say, will the young year dawn with wisdom's light
To brighten o'er thy bier?

Or we the past forget,
And heal her wounds too tenderly to last?
Or let today grow difficult and vast
With traitors unvoiced yet?

Though thou must leave the tear,--
Hearts bleeding ere they break in silence yet,
Wrong jubilant and right with bright eye wet,--
Thou fast expiring year,

Thy work is done, and well:
Thou hast borne burdens, and may take thy rest,
Pillow thy head on time's untired breast.
Illustrious year, farewell!

Lynn, Mass., *January 1, 1866*.

INVOCATION FOR 1868

Father of every age,
Of every rolling sphere,
Help us to write a deathless page
Of truth, this dawning year!

Help us to humbly bow
To Thy all-wise behest--
Whate'er the gift of joy or woe,
Knowing Thou knowest best.

Aid our poor soul to sing
Above the tempest's glee;
Give us the eagle's fearless wing,
The dove's to soar to Thee!

All-merciful and good,
Hover the homeless heart!
Give us this day our daily food
In knowing what Thou art!

Swampscott, Mass., *January 1, 1868*.

CHRISTMAS MORN

Blest Christmas morn, though murky clouds
Pursue thy way,
Thy light was born where storm enshrouds
Nor dawn nor day!

Dear Christ, forever here and near,
No cradle song,
No natal hour and mother's tear,
To thee belong.

Thou God-idea, Life-encrowned,
The Bethlehem babe--
Beloved, replete, by flesh embound--
Was but thy shade!

Thou gentle beam of living Love,
And deathless Life!
Truth infinite,--so far above
All mortal strife,

Or cruel creed, or earth-born taint:
Fill us today
With all thou art--be thou our saint,
Our stay, alway.

December, 1898.

EASTER MORN

Gently thou beckonest from the giant hills
The new-born beauty in the emerald sky,
And wakening murmurs from the drowsy rills--
O gladsome dayspring! 'reft of mortal sigh
To glorify all time--eternity--
With thy still fathomless Christ-majesty.

E'en as Thou gildest gladdened joy, dear God,
Give risen power to prayer; fan Thou the flame
Of right with might; and midst the rod,
And stern, dark shadows cast on Thy blest name,
Lift Thou a patient love above earth's ire,
Piercing the clouds with its triumphal spire.

While sacred song and loudest breath of praise
Echo amid the hymning spheres of light,--
With heaven's lyres and angels' loving lays,--
Send to the loyal struggler for the right,
Joy--not of time, nor yet by nature sown,
But the celestial seed dropped from Love's throne.

Prolong the strain "Christ risen!" Sad sense, annoy
No more the peace of Soul's sweet solitude!
Deep loneness, tear-filled tones of distant joy,
Depart! Glad Easter glows with gratitude--
Love's verdure veils the leaflet's wondrous birth--
Rich rays, rare footprints on the dust of earth.

Not life, the vassal of the changeful hour,

Nor burdened bliss, but Truth and Love attest
The solemn splendor of immortal power,--
The ever Christ, and glorified behest,
Poured on the sense which deems no suffering vain
That wipes away the sting of death--sin, pain.

Pleasant View, Concord, N. H., *April 18, 1900*.

RESOLUTIONS FOR THE DAY

To rise in the morning and drink in the view--
The home where I dwell in the vale,
The blossoms whose fragrance and charms ever new
Are scattered o'er hillside and dale;

To gaze on the sunbeams enkindling the sky--
A loftier life to invite--
A light that illumines my spiritual eye,
And inspires my pen as I write;

To form resolutions, with strength from on high,
Such physical laws to obey,
As reason with appetite, pleasures deny,
That health may my efforts repay;

To kneel at the altar of mercy and pray
That pardon and grace, through His Son,
May comfort my soul all the wearisome day,
And cheer me with hope when 'tis done;

To daily remember my blessings and charge,
And make this my humble request:
Increase Thou my faith and my vision enlarge,
And bless me with Christ's promised rest;

To hourly seek for deliverance strong
From selfishness, sinfulness, dearth,
From vanity, folly, and all that is wrong--
With ambition that binds us to earth;

To kindly pass over a wound, or a foe
(And mem'ry but part us awhile),
To breathe forth a prayer that His love I may know,
Whose mercies my sorrows beguile,--

If these resolutions are acted up to,
And faith spreads her pinions abroad,
'Twill be sweet when I ponder the days may be few
That waft me away to my God.

Written in girlhood.

O FOR THY WINGS, SWEET BIRD!

O for thy wings, sweet bird!
And soul of melody by being blest--
Like thee, my voice had stirred
Some dear remembrance in a weary breast.

But whither wouldst thou rove,
Bird of the airy wing, and fold thy plumes?
In what dark leafy grove
Wouldst chant thy vespers 'mid rich glooms?

Or sing thy love-lorn note--
In deeper solitude, where nymph or saint
Has wooed some mystic spot,
Divinely desolate the shrine to paint?

Yet wherefore ask thy doom?
Blessed compared with me thou art--
Unto thy greenwood home
Bearing no bitter memory at heart;

Wearing no earthly chain,
Thou canst in azure bright soar far above;
Nor pinest thou in vain
O'er joys departed, unforgotten love.

O take me to thy bower!
Beguile the lagging hours of weariness
With strain which hath strange power
To make me love thee as I love life less!

From mortal consciousness
Which binds to earth--infirmity of woe!
Or pining tenderness--
Whose streams will never dry or cease to flow;

An aching, voiceless void,
Hushed in the heart whereunto none reply,

And in the cringing crowd
Companionless! Bird, bear me through the sky!

Written more than sixty years ago for the *New Hampshire Patriot*.

COME THOU

Come, in the minstrel's lay;
When two hearts meet,
And true hearts greet,
And all is morn and May.

Come Thou! and now, anew,
To thought and deed
Give sober speed,
Thy will to know, and do.

Stay! till the storms are o'er--
The cold blasts done,
The reign of heaven begun,
And Love, the evermore.

Be patient, waiting heart:
Light, Love divine
Is here, and thine;
You therefore cannot part.

"The seasons come and go:
Love, like the sea,

Rolls on with thee,--
But knows no ebb and flow.

"Faith, hope, and tears, triune,
Above the sod
Find peace in God,
And one eternal noon."

Oh, Thou hast heard my prayer;
And I am blest!
This is Thy high behest:
Thou, here and ***everywhere***.

WISH AND ITEM

To the editor of the ***Item***, Lynn, Mass.

I hope the heart that's hungry
For things above the floor,
Will find within its portals
An item rich in store;

That melancholy mortals
Will count their mercies o'er,
And learn that Truth and wisdom
Have many items more;

That when a wrong is done us,
It stirs no thought of strife;

And Love becomes the substance,
As item, of our life;

That every ragged urchin,
With bare feet soiled or sore,
Share God's most tender mercies,--
Find items at our door.

Then if we've done to others
Some good ne'er told before,
When angels shall repeat it,
'Twill be an item more.

DEDICATION OF A TEMPERANCE HALL

Author of all divine
Gifts, lofty, pure, and free,
Temperance and truth in song sublime
An offering bring to Thee!

A temple, whose high dome
Rose from a water-cup;
And from its altar to Thy throne
May we press on and up!

And she--last at the cross,
First at the tomb, who waits--
Woman--will watch to cleanse from dross
The cause she elevates.

Sons of the old Bay State,
Work for our glorious cause!
And be your waiting hearts elate,
Since temperance makes your laws.

"Temples of Honor," all,
"Social," or grand, or great,
This blazoned, brilliant temperance hall
To Thee we dedicate.

"Good Templars" one and all,
Good "Sons," and daughters, too,
We dedicate this temperance hall
To God, to Truth, and you!

Lynn, Mass., *August 4, 1866*.

LINES

Come, rest in this bosom, my own stricken deer.--*Moore.*

Was that fold for the lambkin soft virtue's repose,
Where the weary and earth-stricken lay down their woes,--
When the fountain and leaflet are frozen and sere,
And the mountains more friendless,--their home is not here?

When the herd had forsaken, and left them to stray
From the green sunny slopes of the woodland away;
Where the music of waters had fled to the sea,

And this life but one given to suffer and be?

Was it then thou didst call them to banish all pain,
And the harpstring, just breaking, reecho again
To a strain of enchantment that flowed as the wave,
Where they waited to welcome the murmur it gave?

Oh, there's never a shadow where sunshine is not,
And never the sunshine without a dark spot;
Yet there's one will be victor, for glory and fame,
Without heart to define them, were only a name!

Lynn, Mass., *February 19, 1868*.

TO THE SUNDAY SCHOOL CHILDREN

Who sent me the picture depictive of Isaiah xi.

Jesus loves you! so does mother:
Glad thy Eastertide:
Loving God and one another,
You in Him abide.
Ours through Him who gave you to us,--
Gentle as the dove,
Fondling e'en the lion furious,
Leading kine with love.

Father, in Thy great heart hold them
Ever thus as Thine!

Shield and guide and guard them; and, when
At some siren shrine
They would lay their pure hearts' off'ring,
Light with wisdom's ray--
Beacon beams--athwart the weakly,
Rough or treacherous way.

Temper every trembling footfall,
Till they gain at last--
Safe in Science, bright with glory--
Just the way Thou hast:
Then, O tender Love and wisdom,
Crown the lives thus blest
With the guerdon of Thy bosom,
Whereon they may rest!

Pleasant View, Concord, N. H., *April 3, 1899*.

HOPE

Tis borne on the zephyr at eventide's hour;
It falls on the heart like the dew on the flower,--
An infinite essence from tropic to pole,
The promise, the home, and the heaven of Soul.

Hope happifies life, at the altar or bower,
And loosens the fetters of pride and of power;
It comes through our tears, as the soft summer rain,
To beautify, bless, and make joyful again.

The harp of the minstrel, the treasure of time;
A rainbow of rapture, o'erarching, divine;
The God-given mandate that speaks from above,--
No place for earth's idols, but hope thou, and love.

TO ETTA

Fair girl, thy rosebud heart rests warm
Within life's summer bowers!
Nor blasts of winter's angry storm,
Nor April's changeful showers,

Its leaves have shed or bowed the stem;
But gracefully it stands--
A gem in beauty's diadem,
Unplucked by ruthless hands.

Thus may it ripen into bloom,
Fresh as the fragrant sod,
And yield its beauty and perfume
An offering pure to God.

Sweet as the poetry of heaven,
Bright as her evening star,
Be all thy life in music given,
While beauty fills each bar.

Lynn, Mass., **December 8, 1866**.

NEVERMORE

Are the dear days ever coming again,
As sweetly they came of yore,
Singing the olden and dainty refrain,
Oh, ever and nevermore?

Ever to gladness and never to tears,
Ever the gross world above;
Never to toiling and never to fears,
Ever to Truth and to Love?

Can the forever of happiness be
Outside this ever of pain?
Will the hereafter from suffering free
The weary of body and brain?

Weary of sobbing, like some tired child
Over the tears it has shed;
Weary of sowing the wayside and wild,
Watching the husbandman fled;

Nevermore reaping the harvest we deem,
Evermore gathering in woe--
Say, are the sheaves and the gladness a dream,
Or to the patient who sow?

Lynn, Mass., *September 3, 1871*.

MEETING OF MY DEPARTED MOTHER AND HUSBAND

Joy for thee, happy friend! thy bark is past
The dangerous sea, and safely moored at last--
Beyond rough foam.
Soft gales celestial, in sweet music bore--
Spirit emancipate for this far shore--
Thee to thy home.

"You've traveled long, and far from mortal joys,
To Soul's diviner sense, that spurns such toys,
Brave wrestler, lone.
Now see thy ever-self; Life never fled;
Man is not mortal, never of the dead:
The dark unknown.

"When hope soared high, and joy was eagle-plumed,
Thy pinions drooped; the flesh was weak, and doomed
To pass away.
But faith triumphant round thy death-couch shed
Majestic forms; and radiant glory sped
The dawning day.

"Intensely grand and glorious life's sphere,--
Beyond the shadow, infinite appear
Life, Love divine,--
Where mortal yearnings come not, sighs are stilled,
And home and peace and hearts are found and filled,

Thine, ever thine.

"Bearest thou no tidings from our loved on earth,
The toiler tireless for Truth's new birth
All-unbeguiled?
Our joy is gathered from her parting sigh:
This hour looks on her heart with pitying eye,--
What of my child?"

"When, severed by death's dream, I woke to Life,
She deemed I died, and could not know the strife
At first to fill
That waking with a love that steady turns
To God; a hope that ever upward yearns,
Bowed to His will.

"Years had passed o'er thy broken household band,
When angels beckoned me to this bright land,
With thee to meet.
She that has wept o'er thee, kissed my cold brow,
Rears the sad marble to our memory now,
In lone retreat.

"By the remembrance of her loyal life,
And parting prayer, I only know my wife,
Thy child, shall come--
Where farewells cloud not o'er our ransomed rest--
Hither to reap, with all the crowned and blest,
Of bliss the sum.

"When Love's rapt sense the heartstrings gently sweep
With joy divinely fair, the high and deep,
To call her home,

She shall mount upward unto purer skies;
We shall be waiting, in what glad surprise,
Our spirits' own!"

ISLE OF WIGHT

On receiving a painting of the Isle.

Isle of beauty, thou art singing
To my sense a sweet refrain;
To my busy mem'ry bringing
Scenes that I would see again.

Chief, the charm of thy reflecting,
Is the moral that it brings;
Nature, with the mind connecting,
Gives the artist's fancy wings.

Soul, sublime 'mid human *debris*,
Paints the limner's work, I ween,
Art and Science, all unweary,
Lighting up this mortal dream.

Work ill-done within the misty
Mine of human thoughts, we see
Soon abandoned when the Master
Crowns life's Cliff for such as we.

Students wise, he maketh now thus

Those who fish in waters deep,
When the buried Master hails us
From the shores afar, complete.

Art hath bathed this isthmus-lordling
In a beauty strong and meek
As the rock, whose upward tending
Points the plane of power to seek.

Isle of beauty, thou art teaching
Lessons long and grand, tonight,
To my heart that would be bleaching
To thy whiteness, Cliff of Wight.

SPRING

Come to thy bowers, sweet spring,
And paint the gray, stark trees,
The bud, the leaf and wing--
Bring with thee brush and breeze.

And soft thy shading lay
On vale and woodland deep;
With sunshine's lovely ray
Light o'er the rugged steep.

More softly warm and weave
The patient, timid grass,
Till heard at silvery eve

Poor robin's lonely mass.

Bid faithful swallows come
And build their cozy nests,
Where wind nor storm can numb
Their downy little breasts.

Come at the sad heart's call,
To empty summer bowers,
Where still and dead are all
The vernal songs and flowers.

It may be months or years
Since joyous spring was there.
O come to clouds and tears
With light and song and prayer!

JUNE

Whence are thy wooings, gentle June?
Thou hast a naiad's charm;
Thy breezes scent the rose's breath;
Old Time gives thee her palm.
The lark's shrill song doth wake the dawn:
The eve-bird's forest flute
Gives back some maiden melody,
Too pure for aught so mute.

The fairy-peopled world of flowers,

Enraptured by thy spell,
Looks love unto the laughing hours,
Through woodland, grove, and dell;
And soft thy footstep falls upon
The verdant grass it weaves;
To melting murmurs ye have stirred
The timid, trembling leaves.

When sunshine beautifies the shower,
As smiles through teardrops seen,
Ask of its June, the long-hushed heart,
What hath the record been?
And thou wilt find that harmonies,
In which the Soul hath part,
Ne'er perish young, like things of earth,
In records of the heart.

RONDELET

The flowers of June
The gates of memory unbar:
The flowers of June
Such old-time harmonies retune,
I fain would keep the gates ajar,--
So full of sweet enchantment are
The flowers of June.

--*James T. White.*

Who loves not June
Is out of tune
With love and God;
The rose his rival reigns,
The stars reject his pains,
His home the clod!

And yet I trow,
When sweet *rondeau*
Doth play a part,
The curtain drops on June;
Veiled is the modest moon--
Hushed is the heart.

AUTUMN

Quickly earth's jewels disappear;
The turf, whereon I tread,
Ere autumn blanch another year,
May rest above my head.

Touched by the finger of decay
Is every earthly love;
For joy, to shun my weary way,
Is registered above.

The languid brooklets yield their sighs,
A requiem o'er the tomb
Of sunny days and cloudless skies,

Enhancing autumn's gloom.

The wild winds mutter, howl, and moan,
To scare my woodland walk,
And frightened fancy flees, to roam
Where ghosts and goblins stalk.

The cricket's sharp, discordant scream
Fills mortal sense with dread;
More sorrowful it scarce could seem;
It voices beauty fled.

Yet here, upon this faded sod,--
O happy hours and fleet,--
When songsters' matin hymns to God
Are poured in strains so sweet,

My heart unbidden joins rehearse,
I hope it's better made,
When mingling with the universe,
Beneath the maple's shade.

Written in girlhood, in a maple grove.

ALPHABET AND BAYONET

If fancy plumes aerial flight,
Go fix thy restless mind
On learning's lore and wisdom's might,

And live to bless mankind.
The sword is sheathed, 'tis freedom's hour,
No despot bears misrule,
Where knowledge plants the foot of power
In our God-blessed free school.

Forth from this fount the streamlets flow,
That widen in their course.
Hero and sage arise to show
Science the mighty source,
And laud the land whose talents rock
The cradle of her power,
And wreaths are twined round Plymouth Rock,
From erudition's bower.

Farther than feet of chamois fall,
Free as the generous air,
Strains nobler far than clarion call
Wake freedom's welcome, where
Minerva's silver sandals still
Are loosed, and not effete;
Where echoes still my day-dreams thrill,
Woke by her fancied feet.

THE COUNTRY-SEAT

Wild spirit of song,--midst the zephyrs at play
In bowers of beauty,--I bend to thy lay,
And woo, while I worship in deep sylvan spot,

The Muses' soft echoes to kindle the grot.
Wake chords of my lyre, with musical kiss,
To vibrate and tremble with accents of bliss.

Here morning peers out, from her crimson repose,
On proud Prairie Queen and the modest Moss-rose;
And vesper reclines--when the dewdrop is shed
On the heart of the pink--in its odorous bed;
But Flora has stolen the rainbow and sky,
To sprinkle the flowers with exquisite dye.

Here fame-honored hickory rears his bold form,
And bares a brave breast to the lightning and storm,
While palm, bay, and laurel, in classical glee,
Chase tulip, magnolia, and fragrant fringe-tree;
And sturdy horse-chestnut for centuries hath given
Its feathery blossom and branches to heaven.

Here is life! Here is youth! Here the poet's world-wish,--
Cool waters at play with the gold-gleaming fish;
While cactus a mellower glory receives
From light colored softly by blossom and leaves;
And nestling alder is whispering low,
In lap of the pear-tree, with musical flow.[1]

Dark sentinel hedgerow is guarding repose,
Midst grotto and songlet and streamlet that flows
Where beauty and perfume from buds burst away,
And ope their closed cells to the bright, laughing day;
Yet, dwellers in Eden, earth yields you her tear,--
Oft plucked for the banquet, but laid on the bier.

Earth's beauty and glory delude as the shrine

Or fount of real joy and of visions divine;
But hope, as the eaglet that spurneth the sod,
May soar above matter, to fasten on God,
And freely adore all His spirit hath made,
Where rapture and radiance and glory ne'er fade.

Oh, give me the spot where affection may dwell
In sacred communion with home's magic spell!
Where flowers of feeling are fragrant and fair,
And those we most love find a happiness rare;
But clouds are a presage,--they darken my lay:
This life is a shadow, and hastens away.

[1] An alder growing from the bent branch of a pear-tree.

TO ELLEN. "SING ME THAT SONG!"

Sing me that song! My spirit is sad,
Life's pulses move fitful and slow;
A meeting with loved ones in dreams I have had,
Whose robes were as spotless as snow:
A phantom of joy, it fled with the light,
And left but a parting in air.
My soul is enchained to life's dreary night,
O sing me "Sweet hour of prayer"!

Ah, sleep, twin sister of death and of night!
My thoughts 'neath thy drap'ry still lie.
Alas! that from dreams so boundless and bright

We waken to life's dreary sigh.
Those moments most sweet are fleetest alway,
For love claspeth earth's raptures not long,
Till darkness and death like mist melt away,
To rise to a seraph's new song.

O'er ocean or Alps, the stranger who roams
But gathers a wreath for his bier;
For life hath its music in low minor tones,
And *man* is the cause of its tear.
But drops of pure nectar our brimming cup fill,
When we walk by that murmuring stream;
Or when, like the thrill of that mountain rill,
Your songs float in memory's dream.

Sweet spirit of love, at soft eventide
Wake gently the chords of her lyre,
And whisper of one who sat by her side
To join with the neighboring choir;
And tell how that heart is silent and sad,
No melody sweeps o'er its strings!
'Tis breaking alone, but a young heart and glad--
Might cheer it, perchance, when she sings.

Lynn, Mass., *August 25, 1866*.

LINES, ON VISITING PINE GROVE CEMETERY

Ah, why should the brief bliss of life's little day

Grow cold in this spot as the spiritless clay,
And thought be at work with the long-buried hours,
And tears be bedewing these fresh-smiling flowers!

Ah, wherefore the memory of dear ones deemed dead
Should bow thee, as winds bow the tall willow's head!
Beside you they walk while you weep, and but pass
From your sight as the shade o'er the dark wavy grass.

The cypress may mourn with her evergreen tears,
And, like the blue hyacinth, change not with years;
Yea, flowers of feeling may blossom above,
To yield earth the fragrance of goodness and love;

So one heart is left me--she breathes in my ear,
"I'm living to bless thee; for this are we here."
And when this sweet pledge to my lone heart was given,
Earth held but this joy, or this happiness heaven!

Here the rock and the sea and the tall waving pine
Enchant deep the senses,--subduing, sublime;
Yet stronger than these is the spell that hath power
To sweep o'er the heartstrings in memory's hour.

Of the past 'tis the talisman, when ***we three met***,
When the star of our friendship arose not to set;
And pure as its rising, and bright as the star,
Be its course through our heavens, whether near or afar.

Lynn, Mass., **August 24, 1865**.

A VERSE

Mother's New Year Gift to the Little Children

> Father-Mother God,
> Loving me,--
> Guard me when I sleep;
> Guide my little feet
> Up to Thee.

To the Big Children

> Father-Mother good, lovingly
> Thee I seek,--
> Patient, meek,
> In the way Thou hast,--
> Be it slow or fast,
> Up to Thee.

TRUTH

> Beyond the clouds, away
> In the dim distance, lay
> A bright and golden shower
> At sunset's radiant hour,--

Like to the soul's glad immortality,
Making this life divine,
Making its waters wine,
Giving the glory that eye cannot see.

In God there is no night,--
Truth is eternal light,
A help forever near;
For sinless sense is here
In Truth, the Life, the Principle of man.
Away, then, mortal sense!
Then, error, get thee hence,
Thy discord ne'er in harmony began!

Immortal Truth,--since heaven rang,
The while the glad stars sang
To hail creation's glorious morn--
As when this babe was born,
A painless heraldry of Soul, not sense,--
Shine on our 'wildered way,
Give God's idea sway,
And sickness, sin, and death are banished hence.

Lynn, Mass., *April, 1871*.

"*THE LIBERTY BELLS*"

This is the hour they then foretold--
When earth, inebriate with crime,

Laughed right to scorn, and guilt, grown bold,
Knelt worshiping at mammon's shrine.

This is the hour! Corruption's band
Is driven back; and periled right,
Rescued by the "fanatic" hand,
Spans our broad heaven of light.

Righteousness ne'er--awestruck or dumb--
Feared for an hour the tyrant's heel!
Injustice to the combat sprang;
God to the rescue--Liberty, peal!

Joy is in every belfry bell--
Joy for the captive! Sound it long!
Ye who have wept fourscore can tell
The holy meaning of their song.

'Tis freedom's birthday--blood-bought boon!
O war-rent flag! O soldier-shroud!
Thine be the glory--nor too soon
Is heard your "Cry aloud!"

O not too soon is rent the chain
And charter, trampling right in dust!
Till God is God no longer--ne'er again
Quench liberty that's just.

Lynn, Mass., **February 3, 1865**.

"*MEMENTO*"

Respectfully inscribed to my friends in Lynn.

I come to thee
O'er the moonlit sea,
When the hoarse wave revisits thy shore!
When waters shout,
And the stars peep out,
I am with thee in spirit once more.

Then list the moan
Of the billows' foam,
Laving with surges thy silv'ry beach!
Night's dewy eye,
The sea-mew's lone cry,
Witness my presence and utter my speech.

Pleasant a grave
By the "Rock" or wave,
And afar from life's turmoil its goal.
No sculptured lie,
Or hypocrite sigh,
E'er to mock the bright truth of the soul.

Friends, will not ye
Think kindly of me,
In those moments to memory bestowed?
Smile on me yet,
O blue eyes and jet,
Soft as when parting thy sympathy glowed!

March 3, 1867.

COMMUNION HYMN

Saw ye my Saviour? Heard ye the glad sound?
Felt ye the power of the Word?
'Twas the Truth that made us free,
And was found by you and me
In the life and the love of our Lord.

Mourner, it calls you,--"Come to my bosom,
Love wipes your tears all away,
And will lift the shade of gloom,
And for you make radiant room
Midst the glories of one endless day."

Sinner, it calls you,--"Come to this fountain,
Cleanse the foul senses within;
'Tis the Spirit that makes pure,
That exalts thee, and will cure
All thy sorrow and sickness and sin."

Strongest deliverer, friend of the friendless,
Life of all being divine:
Thou the Christ, and not the creed;
Thou the Truth in thought and deed;
Thou the water, the bread, and the wine.

LAUS DEO!

The laying of the corner-stone of The Mother Church.

Laus Deo, it is done!
Rolled away from loving heart
Is a stone.
Lifted higher, we depart,
Having one.

Laus Deo,--on this rock
(Heaven chiseled squarely good)
Stands His church,--
God is Love, and understood
By His flock.

Laus Deo, night star-lit
Slumbers not in God's embrace;
Be awake;
Like this stone, be in thy place:
Stand, not sit.

Grave, silent, steadfast stone,
Dirge and song and shoutings low
In thy heart
Dwell serene,--and sorrow? No,
It has none,
Laus Deo!

OUR NATIONAL THANKSGIVING HYMN

God of the rolling year! to Thee we raise
A nation's holiest hymn in grateful praise!
Plenty and peace abound at Thy behest,
Yet wherefore this Thy love? Thou knowest best!

Thou who, impartial, blessings spreadst abroad,
Thou wisdom, Love, and Truth,--divinely God!
Who giveth joy and tears, conflict and rest,
Teaching us thus of Thee, who knowest best!

Ruler Supreme! to Thee we'll meekly bow,
When we have learned of Truth what Thou doest now--
Why from this festive hour some dear lost guest
Bears hence its sunlit glow--Thou knowest best!

How have our honored dead fought on in gloom!
Peace her white wings will spread over their tomb;
Why waited their reward, triumph and rest,
Till molds the hero form? Thou knowest best!

Shades of our heroes! the Union now is one,
The star whose destiny none may outrun;
Tears of the bleeding slave poured on her breast,
When to be wiped away, Thou knowest best!

Thou who in the Christ hallowed its grief,--
O meekest of mourners, while yet the chief,--

Give to the pleading hearts comfort and rest,
In that benediction which knoweth best!

Lynn, Mass., *December 7, 1865*.

SATISFIED

It matters not what be thy lot,
So Love doth guide;
For storm or shine, pure peace is thine,
Whate'er betide.

And of these stones, or tyrants' thrones,
God able is
To raise up seed--in thought and deed--
To faithful His.

Aye, darkling sense, arise, go hence!
Our God is good.
False fears are foes--truth tatters those,
When understood.

Love looseth thee, and lifteth me,
Ayont hate's thrall:
There Life is light, and wisdom might,
And God is All.

The centuries break, the earth-bound wake,
God's glorified!

Who doth His will--His likeness still--
Is satisfied.

Pleasant View, Concord, N. H., *January, 1900*.

www.bookjungle.com *email: sales@bookjungle.com fax: 630-214-0564 mail: Book Jungle PO Box 2226 Champaign, IL 61825*

The Codes Of Hammurabi And Moses
W. W. Davies

QTY

The discovery of the Hammurabi Code is one of the greatest achievements of archaeology, and is of paramount interest, not only to the student of the Bible, but also to all those interested in ancient history...

Religion   **ISBN:** *1-59462-338-4*   Pages:132
MSRP $12.95

The Theory of Moral Sentiments
Adam Smith

QTY

This work from 1749. contains original theories of conscience amd moral judgment and it is the foundation for systemof morals.

Philosophy   **ISBN:** *1-59462-777-0*   Pages:536
MSRP $19.95

Jessica's First Prayer
Hesba Stretton

QTY

In a screened and secluded corner of one of the many railway-bridges which span the streets of London there could be seen a few years ago, from five o'clock every morning until half past eight, a tidily set-out coffee-stall, consisting of a trestle and board, upon which stood two large tin cans, with a small fire of charcoal burning under each so as to keep the coffee boiling during the early hours of the morning when the work-people were thronging into the city on their way to their daily toil...

Childrens   **ISBN:** *1-59462-373-2*   Pages:84
MSRP $9.95

My Life and Work
Henry Ford

QTY

Henry Ford revolutionized the world with his implementation of mass production for the Model T automobile. Gain valuable business insight into his life and work with his own auto-biography... "We have only started on our development of our country we have not as yet, with all our talk of wonderful progress, done more than scratch the surface. The progress has been wonderful enough but..."

Biographies/   **ISBN:** *1-59462-198-5*   Pages:300
MSRP $21.95

www.bookjungle.com *email: sales@bookjungle.com fax: 630-214-0564 mail: Book Jungle PO Box 2226 Champaign, IL 61825*

The Art of Cross-Examination
Francis Wellman

QTY

I presume it is the experience of every author, after his first book is published upon an important subject, to be almost overwhelmed with a wealth of ideas and illustrations which could readily have been included in his book, and which to his own mind, at least, seem to make a second edition inevitable. Such certainly was the case with me; and when the first edition had reached its sixth impression in five months, I rejoiced to learn that it seemed to my publishers that the book had met with a sufficiently favorable reception to justify a second and considerably enlarged edition. ..

Reference   ISBN: *1-59462-647-2*   Pages:412 *MSRP $19.95*

On the Duty of Civil Disobedience
Henry David Thoreau

QTY

Thoreau wrote his famous essay, On the Duty of Civil Disobedience, as a protest against an unjust but popular war and the immoral but popular institution of slave-owning. He did more than write—he declined to pay his taxes, and was hauled off to gaol in consequence. Who can say how much this refusal of his hastened the end of the war and of slavery ?

Law   ISBN: *1-59462-747-9*   Pages:48 *MSRP $7.45*

Dream Psychology Psychoanalysis for Beginners
Sigmund Freud

QTY

Sigmund Freud, born Sigismund Schlomo Freud (May 6, 1856 - September 23, 1939), was a Jewish-Austrian neurologist and psychiatrist who co-founded the psychoanalytic school of psychology. Freud is best known for his theories of the unconscious mind, especially involving the mechanism of repression; his redefinition of sexual desire as mobile and directed towards a wide variety of objects; and his therapeutic techniques, especially his understanding of transference in the therapeutic relationship and the presumed value of dreams as sources of insight into unconscious desires.

Psychology   ISBN: *1-59462-905-6*   Pages:196 *MSRP $15.45*

The Miracle of Right Thought
Orison Swett Marden

QTY

Believe with all of your heart that you will do what you were made to do. When the mind has once formed the habit of holding cheerful, happy, prosperous pictures, it will not be easy to form the opposite habit. It does not matter how improbable or how far away this realization may see, or how dark the prospects may be, if we visualize them as best we can, as vividly as possible, hold tenaciously to them and vigorously struggle to attain them, they will gradually become actualized, realized in the life. But a desire, a longing without endeavor, a yearning abandoned or held indifferently will vanish without realization.

Self Help   ISBN: *1-59462-644-8*   Pages:360 *MSRP $25.45*

www.bookjungle.com email: sales@bookjungle.com fax: 630-214-0564 mail: Book Jungle PO Box 2226 Champaign, IL 61825

QTY

☐ **The Rosicrucian Cosmo-Conception Mystic Christianity** by **Max Heindel** ISBN: *1-59462-188-8* **$38.95**
The Rosicrucian Cosmo-conception is not dogmatic, neither does it appeal to any other authority than the reason of the student. It is: not controversial, but is: sent forth in the, hope that it may help to clear... New Age/Religion Pages 646

☐ **Abandonment To Divine Providence** by **Jean-Pierre de Caussade** ISBN: *1-59462-228-0* **$25.95**
"The Rev. Jean Pierre de Caussade was one of the most remarkable spiritual writers of the Society of Jesus in France in the 18th Century. His death took place at Toulouse in 1751. His works have gone through many editions and have been republished... Inspirational/Religion Pages 400

☐ **Mental Chemistry** by **Charles Haanel** ISBN: *1-59462-192-6* **$23.95**
Mental Chemistry allows the change of material conditions by combining and appropriately utilizing the power of the mind. Much like applied chemistry creates something new and unique out of careful combinations of chemicals the mastery of mental chemistry... New Age Pages 354

☐ **The Letters of Robert Browning and Elizabeth Barret Barrett 1845-1846 vol II** ISBN: *1-59462-193-4* **$35.95**
by **Robert Browning** and **Elizabeth Barrett** Biographies Pages 596

☐ **Gleanings In Genesis (volume I)** by **Arthur W. Pink** ISBN: *1-59462-130-6* **$27.45**
Appropriately has Genesis been termed "the seed plot of the Bible" for in it we have, in germ form, almost all of the great doctrines which are afterwards fully developed in the books of Scripture which follow... Religion/Inspirational Pages 420

☐ **The Master Key** by **L. W. de Laurence** ISBN: *1-59462-001-6* **$30.95**
In no branch of human knowledge has there been a more lively increase of the spirit of research during the past few years than in the study of Psychology, Concentration and Mental Discipline. The requests for authentic lessons in Thought Control, Mental Discipline and... New Age/Business Pages 422

☐ **The Lesser Key Of Solomon Goetia** by **L. W. de Laurence** ISBN: *1-59462-092-X* **$9.95**
This translation of the first book of the "Lernegton" which is now for the first time made accessible to students of Talismanic Magic was done, after careful collation and edition, from numerous Ancient Manuscripts in Hebrew, Latin, and French... New Age/Occult Pages 92

☐ **Rubaiyat Of Omar Khayyam** by **Edward Fitzgerald** ISBN:*1-59462-332-5* **$13.95**
Edward Fitzgerald, whom the world has already learned, in spite of his own efforts to remain within the shadow of anonymity, to look upon as one of the rarest poets of the century, was born at Bredfield, in Suffolk, on the 31st of March, 1809. He was the third son of John Purcell... Music Pages 172

☐ **Ancient Law** by **Henry Maine** ISBN: *1-59462-128-4* **$29.95**
The chief object of the following pages is to indicate some of the earliest ideas of mankind, as they are reflected in Ancient Law, and to point out the relation of those ideas to modern thought. Religiom/History Pages 452

☐ **Far-Away Stories** by **William J. Locke** ISBN: *1-59462-129-2* **$19.45**
"Good wine needs no bush, but a collection of mixed vintages does. And this book is just such a collection. Some of the stories I do not want to remain buried for ever in the museum files of dead magazine-numbers an author's not unpardonable vanity..." Fiction Pages 272

☐ **Life of David Crockett** by **David Crockett** ISBN: *1-59462-250-7* **$27.45**
"Colonel David Crockett was one of the most remarkable men of the times in which he lived. Born in humble life, but gifted with a strong will, an indomitable courage, and unremitting perseverance... Biographies/New Age Pages 424

☐ **Lip-Reading** by **Edward Nitchie** ISBN: *1-59462-206-X* **$25.95**
Edward B. Nitchie, founder of the New York School for the Hard of Hearing, now the Nitchie School of Lip-Reading, Inc, wrote "LIP-READING Principles and Practice". The development and perfecting of this meritorious work on lip-reading was an undertaking... How-to Pages 400

☐ **A Handbook of Suggestive Therapeutics, Applied Hypnotism, Psychic Science** ISBN: *1-59462-214-0* **$24.95**
by **Henry Munro** Health/New Age/Health/Self-help Pages 376

☐ **A Doll's House: and Two Other Plays** by **Henrik Ibsen** ISBN: *1-59462-112-8* **$19.95**
Henrik Ibsen created this classic when in revolutionary 1848 Rome. Introducing some striking concepts in playwriting for the realist genre, this play has been studied the world over. Fiction/Classics/Plays 308

☐ **The Light of Asia** by **sir Edwin Arnold** ISBN: *1-59462-204-3* **$13.95**
In this poetic masterpiece, Edwin Arnold describes the life and teachings of Buddha. The man who was to become known as Buddha to the world was born as Prince Gautama of India but he rejected the worldly riches and abandoned the reigns of power when... Religion/History/Biographies Pages 170

☐ **The Complete Works of Guy de Maupassant** by **Guy de Maupassant** ISBN: *1-59462-157-8* **$16.95**
"For days and days, nights and nights, I had dreamed of that first kiss which was to consecrate our engagement, and I knew not on what spot I should put my lips..." Fiction/Classics Pages 240

☐ **The Art of Cross-Examination** by **Francis L. Wellman** ISBN: *1-59462-309-0* **$26.95**
Written by a renowned trial lawyer, Wellman imparts his experience and uses case studies to explain how to use psychology to extract desired information through questioning. How-to/Science/Reference Pages 408

☐ **Answered or Unanswered?** by **Louisa Vaughan** ISBN: *1-59462-248-5* **$10.95**
Miracles of Faith in China Religion Pages 112

☐ **The Edinburgh Lectures on Mental Science (1909)** by **Thomas** ISBN: *1-59462-008-3* **$11.95**
This book contains the substance of a course of lectures recently given by the writer in the Queen Street Hall, Edinburgh. Its purpose is to indicate the Natural Principles governing the relation between Mental Action and Material Conditions... New Age/Psychology Pages 148

☐ **Ayesha** by **H. Rider Haggard** ISBN: *1-59462-301-5* **$24.95**
Verily and indeed it is the unexpected that happens! Probably if there was one person upon the earth from whom the Editor of this, and of a certain previous history, did not expect to hear again... Classics Pages 380

☐ **Ayala's Angel** by **Anthony Trollope** ISBN: *1-59462-352-X* **$29.95**
The two girls were both pretty, but Lucy who was twenty-one who supposed to be simple and comparatively unattractive, whereas Ayala was credited, as her Bombwhat romantic name might show, with poetic charm and a taste for romance. Ayala when her father died was nineteen... Fiction Pages 484

☐ **The American Commonwealth** by **James Bryce** ISBN: *1-59462-286-8* **$34.45**
An interpretation of American democratic political theory. It examines political mechanics and society from the perspective of Scotsman James Bryce Politics Pages 572

☐ **Stories of the Pilgrims** by **Margaret P. Pumphrey** ISBN: *1-59462-116-0* **$17.95**
This book explores pilgrims religious oppression in England as well as their escape to Holland and eventual crossing to America on the Mayflower, and their early days in New England... History Pages 268

www.bookjungle.com email: sales@bookjungle.com fax: 630-214-0564 mail: Book Jungle PO Box 2226 Champaign, IL 61825

QTY

The Fasting Cure *by Sinclair Upton* ISBN: *1-59462-222-1* **$13.95**
In the Cosmopolitan Magazine for May, 1910, and in the Contemporary Review (London) for April, 1910, I published an article dealing with my experiences in fasting. I have written a great many magazine articles, but never one which attracted so much attention... *New Age/Self Help/Health Pages 164*

Hebrew Astrology *by Sepharial* ISBN: *1-59462-308-2* **$13.45**
In these days of advanced thinking it is a matter of common observation that we have left many of the old landmarks behind and that we are now pressing forward to greater heights and to a wider horizon than that which represented the mind-content of our progenitors... *Astrology Pages 144*

Thought Vibration or The Law of Attraction in the Thought World ISBN: *1-59462-127-6* **$12.95**
by William Walker Atkinson *Psychology/Religion Pages 144*

Optimism *by Helen Keller* ISBN: *1-59462-108-X* **$15.95**
Helen Keller was blind, deaf, and mute since 19 months old, yet famously learned how to overcome these handicaps, communicate with the world, and spread her lectures promoting optimism. An inspiring read for everyone... *Biographies/Inspirational Pages 84*

Sara Crewe *by Frances Burnett* ISBN: *1-59462-360-0* **$9.45**
In the first place, Miss Minchin lived in London. Her home was a large, dull, tall one, in a large, dull square, where all the houses were alike, and all the sparrows were alike, and where all the door-knockers made the same heavy sound... *Childrens/Classic Pages 88*

The Autobiography of Benjamin Franklin *by Benjamin Franklin* ISBN: *1-59462-135-7* **$24.95**
The Autobiography of Benjamin Franklin has probably been more extensively read than any other American historical work, and no other book of its kind has had such ups and downs of fortune. Franklin lived for many years in England, where he was agent... *Biographies/History Pages 332*

Name	
Email	
Telephone	
Address	
City, State ZIP	

☐ Credit Card   ☐ Check / Money Order

Credit Card Number	
Expiration Date	
Signature	

Please Mail to: Book Jungle
PO Box 2226
Champaign, IL 61825
or Fax to: 630-214-0564

ORDERING INFORMATION
web: www.bookjungle.com
email: sales@bookjungle.com
fax: 630-214-0564
mail: Book Jungle PO Box 2226 Champaign, IL 61825
or PayPal to sales@bookjungle.com

Please contact us for bulk discounts

DIRECT-ORDER TERMS

20% Discount if You Order Two or More Books
Free Domestic Shipping!
Accepted: Master Card, Visa, Discover, American Express

www.ingramcontent.com/pod-product-compliance
Lightning Source LLC
Chambersburg PA
CBHW081328040426
42453CB00013B/2338